THE GRACE EFFECT

THE GRACE EFFECT

EFFECT

FROM BROOKLYN TO BOISE

MICHAEL A. BYRON

To my mother, Emma, wife, Parra, daughter, Morgan, Uncle Heywood and Aunt Dorothy, my father, Lowell, Ben and Jannie, my maternal grandparents, Marie and David, my paternal grandparents, Alexander and Parra, my in-laws, and the rest of family.

"From the first page, I was enamored by *The Grace Effect*. Michael brings to light the many experiences from his childhood that have direct lines to his adult working life, family life, and how the people who poured into him as a child continue to impact him today. His humility in giving credit to his 'village', especially so many women that impacted him and have carried this country, is noteworthy. Michael reminds us that every experience is an important one, to always embrace them, and never forget where you come from."

—Abdul M. Omari, Ph.D., Founder/
Principal, AMO Enterprise

"In *The Grace Effect*, Michael Byron does a graceful job of threading deeds and detours together to make an interesting life story, but his focus on relationships, including the 'Salt and Light' collection, leaves an indelible mark. Never forget our daily effect on others."

—Greg Morley, Cultural Competency Thought
Leader and Advisor, and Author of Bond: Belonging
and the Keys to Inclusion and Connection

"Through trial and triumph, Michael A. Byron's *The Grace Effect* serves as a testament to the resilience born from faith, family, and community. His journey reminds us that with grace and determination, we can rise above life's challenges and inspire others to do the same."

—Brianna Birdwell, President, EID Solutions, and Author
of Metamorphosis of Misfortune: A Path to Power

"I so enjoyed reading Michael Byron's book, *The Grace Effect*. It reminds us all that as we go through life's journey, we are profoundly and forever molded and impacted in our early years into adulthood by individuals that gave of themselves unselfishly and without cost to simply ensure that you can and will be all that you are meant to be in life."

—Donna M. Wilson, President of Strategic Intersections LLC, and Author of Behind the Glass Doors

"Michael Byron opens his soul and reveals what it truly means to achieve more than success. His message is about significance, impact and personal value. Anyone who desires to grow into the best version of themselves should read this book! It will change your life!"

— Trudy Bourgeois, recognized thought leader, consultant and coach, author of four leadership books including Equality: Courageous Conversations About Women, Men, and Race to Spark a Diversity and Inclusion Breakthrough

"*The Grace Effect* is one of the most inspirational, motivational, and enjoyable books I have read in quite some time. Michael Byron's story highlights the importance of role models and a loving mother in making wise choices, overcoming obstacles, taking on challenges, and walking by faith. A must-read for anyone desiring to make it, despite the odds against them."

—Keith R. Wyche, Independent Director, Brinks, and Author of Good Is Not Enough

"Michael Byron's book is a heartfelt and deeply inspiring story that reflects the power of faith, resilience, and community. As someone who believes in the importance of representation and celebrating diverse journeys, I find Michael's story incredibly moving. From the streets of Brooklyn to the heights of corporate success, Michael exemplifies how determination and grace can break through even the toughest barriers. His journey speaks to anyone who has faced hardship, reminding us that with faith and perseverance, no dream is too big. If you've ever thought the mountain was too high to climb, read this book. If you ever had a dream and thought it could not materialize, read this book. If you have a passion, but don't know how to turn it into reality, read this book. Within these pages is the inspiration, answers and roadmap that will inspire you to achieve your dreams and your life's purpose. I am honored to know Michael, and I wholeheartedly endorse this powerful testament to the strength of the human spirit and the transformative role that faith and family can play in one's life. His story is not just one of success but also, of a deep spiritual evolution that will resonate with readers from all walks of life."

—Dr. Lisa Williams, Founder & CEO of The Dr. Lisa Brands, home of the Fresh Dolls

"As an accomplished businessman, Michael has written a beautiful book that lets the world know about the grace of God in your life. *The Grace Effect* shows what his mother's love and strong discipline, the village that kept him from harm, and the men of Bed-Stuy who inspired him to greatness could do. From them, Michael learned the importance of giving grace back to others along the way as he climbed to the top. I know because I benefited from it! *The Grace Effect*, indeed. Well-done, my friend."

—Amy S. Hilliard, Founder, Author, Educator, Principal, and International Speaker, The Hilliard Group, ComfortCake Company and Sugarless Sweetness LLC

"In his tenure in large retail, Michael Byron was a dream maker for hundreds of budding entrepreneurs. Now, he is an innovator and inclusive mentor with a lot to say about being a modern change agent and passing it on. He lets us into a little-known world of an iconic retail chain while tracing his steps from Brooklyn to Boise, which are better for his contributions."

—Marcia-Elizabeth C. Favale, Tech Entrepreneur and Inventor, and Author of Leading Innovation and Inclusion *and* Risk, Recovery, and Empowerment: The Kazakhstan Bank Recovery Case Study

FOREWORD

One thing I remember from my childhood was life lessons; "lectures", as some would call it, from my father. They would range in subject from the importance of keeping my room clean, putting my best foot forward (grades, grooming, eye contact and a firm hand shake), seeing something you started through to the end, and never forgetting that someone prayed on your behalf or thought enough to help get you to where you are, so don't forget to pay it forward as you progress in life. Those lectures have become valued life lessons as I have become older. I am now an adult, living on my own and entrusted to forge my own path. I am comfortable and confident in making choices because of the sound advice provided from both my mother and father growing up; I continue to grow through our discussions and the examples they provide even today.

My father has an incredible wealth of knowledge to share, not only from a business perspective, but more importantly, from a life experience perspective. I am overjoyed that he followed God's voice to see this passion project through. As a reader, you will not only glean key points to help you be successful in your career ventures; moreover, you will attain life lessons to carry with you as I have.

"Walk in your purpose and be intentional in your actions," is a quote often ending his emails. Dad, thank you for continuing to walk in your purpose and always being intentional in your service and care of others. I love you.

—*Morgan Camille Byron, M.A., CCC-SLP*

ACKNOWLEDGMENTS

First and foremost, I would like to thank my wife, Parra Lee Byron, for being the strength that I needed, and saving my life. Your support, prayers and steady hand has afforded me an abundant and blessed life. Without you, I wouldn't be here!

I'm eternally grateful for people who have supported my journey, which is the basis for *The Grace Effect*!

Dr. V. Simpson and Laura Turner (Mt Carmel Baptist Church), Deacons Gilchrist and West (Cub and Boy Scout Leaders). Bill Miles (father figure), Community Center leaders (Ms. Barbara and Mr. Johnson), Sam Pothier, Ron Dennis, Patrick Campbell, Rudy and Alice Cannon, Ron and Lena Hawthorne, Ishizu Family, Don and Connie Prince, Kinsella Family, Smart Family, McNary Family, Mitchell Family, McRoberts Family, Susan Morris, Peggy McReynolds, Amy Hilliard, Trudy Bourgeois, Selena Cuffe, Duncan Mac Naughton, Rich Juliano, Roz Brewer, Don Frieson and Doug McMillon, Richelieu Dennis, Andrea McBride John and Robin McBride, Marcus Johnson, and numerous others.

My brothers of Gamma Xi Lambda and Omicron Xi Lambda - Alpha Phi Alpha Fraternity Incorporated, and my LB, Brian McIntosh.

Thank you to my enthusiastic, exceptional editor, Candi S. Cross, whose contact info I saved for when the time was right to tell my story.

CONTENTS

ANSWERING THE CALL FOR INSPIRATIONAL LEADERSHIP

"Through mistakes we've learned to gather wisdom. Life's responsibility falls in our hands."

—*New Edition*

I BELIEVE IT was God's grace for me to live somewhat of a normal life. I now understand the message that was given to me as a young man that if I worked hard, if I participated, if I came with my tools, my ball and bat, that I had as good a chance of succeeding in life as anyone else. I could make it irrespective of the fact that I was raised by a single mother, or our environment was tough and there were obstacles on all four corners surrounding me. I would see people lying in the gutter with injuries that may have occurred the night before due to an altercation or being inebriated from alcohol or heroin and other substances.

I recall seeing a neighbor, who was an alcoholic. He would often be found in the vestibule bloodied and bruised. The occurrence was so regular, I became numb to him. I would just step over my own neighbor and continue with my tasks. The ambulance would eventually come to scoop him up and life would go on. I saw those disturbing things. And even amid all that, because of so many role models, I was able to live a normal life and sleep good at night. I attributed it to the assortment of figures in my life who lived upright, didn't take any nonsense, protected us and protected our neighborhood.

Church was a large part of my shield, my blanket. The church supported me, told me I could be whoever and whatever I wanted to be. Many years later, my pastor was disappointed that after college I didn't come back home to live and work in the community. I think he expected us all to return and do work in the church and pay it forward as it had been done for us as young people. I reassured my pastor that I was paying it forward elsewhere. It was just that my life wasn't in New York anymore.

Once I stated these words, he looked at me differently because he wasn't fully aware of what I was doing, and he hoped that I would be doing good no matter where I lived. Although he would hear from my mother and she would say, "Oh, he's doing fine," he didn't know firsthand. I didn't reach out or ever write letters or call because of the distance and the time that we had been separated by.

As I continued to grow into adulthood and leadership, he was reassured that I was doing my part to pay it forward, passing the grace effect on. He simply wanted me to be around to pour back into the next generation at our church back in Bed-Stuy. I believe he would have been proud of how I poured into so many people through direct and indirect mentoring, recruitment, teammates, employees, sponsorship, philanthropy, and through my dear fraternity, Alpha Phi Alpha Inc. One thing about me you will learn—I would have been doing that kind of work no matter where I lived in the country. And there would be many marvelous, colorful places, where we flourished as family.

There were so many inspiring people in the places that I worked who didn't look like me. Respect, empathetic engagement, heartful connection were natural qualities and behaviors for me when it came to interacting with others, no matter what they looked like. This sprouted from the early days of being bused to school from Bed-Stuy to Ridgewood, Queens.

Going to that school and eventually being welcomed by my classmates, them not feeling afraid of me and me not afraid of them, gave me a solid foundation, along with working in places like top department stores and the library back in Brooklyn. Most inner-city youth were not exposed to or presented with these types of opportunities and experiences.

As I began editing and polishing the final pages of this book, I lost a friend, who I had just spent time with, to cancer. His death sparked instant questions for me to consider: How do you live now? How do you celebrate the lives of people you loved, admired and who had a direct impact on your personal and professional life? Honoring what my pastor wished for me. I needed to keep pouring good stuff into the next generation and whomever I came in contact with, along with those willing to receive what I had experienced on my life's journey.

Profound losses helped me be a better husband, father, mentor, and all-around human being because it allowed me to hold myself accountable with them on my shoulders. When I remember those losses, I find myself in tears, but they're mainly tears of joy from the memories and meaning. They refresh me. Crying is healthy. This raw expression reminds you that you are blessed enough to be alive and serving others.

CHAPTER 1

BED-STUY, DO OR DIE

"Give light and people will find the way."
—*Ella Baker, human rights activist*

I WAS BORN in the Bed-Stuy section of Brooklyn, New York, raised by a single mother, in the late 60s and 70s. In fact, Bed-Stuy boasted a sort of mantra, "Bed-Stuy, do or die." When I was growing up, it felt like you would either do or you die, but it really wasn't about that. It was about perseverance—and our ability to rise above the degradation that was in the community. At the time, young, Black and Brown men were not supposed to live past twenty-one years of age. If they did, they would either be tangled in the justice or foster system addicted to drugs or worse, homeless on the streets. A sort of numbness lingered in the atmosphere back then because we were shielded until we read the newspaper announcements or caught sight of the funeral down the block. When death knocked on the door of your own family, then it would be felt and seep through your system. Melancholy would be a constant companion. However, life would go on until the next tragedy or incident in neighborhood. It's surreal to think we continued living and thriving despite life's extreme uncertainty hour to hour. I guess it was our youth and inexperience that readied us for whatever was next.

My mother was nineteen years old when she arrived in New York from Florida. She worked hard. Often, she worked two jobs to keep a roof over our head. I feel very fortunate that my mother raised me, even though she was a tough parent. I did fear her but not in the sense of shivering in terror. A fear of disappointing her would probably be more apropos. She gave me a sense of purpose, honor, and integrity. I recall watching her walk in the snow and ice for many years to take the bus before she ever purchased a car, which was unacceptable to me. As a man, there was no alternative but for me to figure out how to work and make my own way, as well as ease my mother's burden.

In New York, some of us call our mothers "Mommy", some of us call our mothers "Mom". I affectionately called my mother "Ma". I remember her start in a factory, making suitcases on an assembly line. She worked every day, well or unwell. At Christmas, she worked two jobs to make sure there were gifts for me under the tree. Whatever she did, she approached it with pride. She dressed in heels, made up her face and *showed up* to the factory.

For the first thirteen years of my life, that's what Ma did until the pastor of our church got her enrolled in a training program, which she mastered. Ma earned a certificate of completion, which enabled her to land a better-paying job with benefits and a career opportunity. Chase Manhattan Bank was one of the larger banks in New York at that time. She went on to work there for nearly three and half decades, climbing the ladder with her high heels. I was exceptionally proud of my mom every day.

She told me a lot of stories of being in the finance industry and training many men and women, who became her bosses. Ma advanced as a vice president in lending and bonding—she was grateful for her roles and never complained. If anything, she was proud to have trained the men and women, wearing it as a sort of badge of honor! Simultaneously, Ma has always maintained her deep faith. She will not miss a Sunday session of church nor her activities as a volunteer at least twice a week. She taught me the grace effect—that there would never be an insurmountable problem because of our efforts and the grace of God. Today, whenever I'm addressing a group of women, I talk about my mother first and foremost, then the rest of the "women in my life who told me what to do—and I listened!"

I went to daycare through extended family, Ms. Cora, from the time I was two. She was very nurturing. I remember the ample food and hugs! Ms. Cora's son was a bit of a street guy, a hustler, so I picked up some unsavory things from him. For example, repeating phrases in front of my mom like "shoot dice from two pennies…Mama needs a brand-new dress…come on, baby!" Then once when getting ice cream and the landlord asking me why I didn't bring him any, as I fumbled with all the sweetness, I replied, "Because I didn't have any damned money!" My mother blushed, but he laughed so hard, she thought he would tumble down the hallway stairs.

I discovered as you grow older, you had to have intuition and discernment about yourself when walking the streets of any inner city. Even if you were only seven or eight years old, somebody would likely try to intimidate or take advantage of you. You had no idea what might happen. So, you had to walk with your head up and be very cognizant of people walking towards you, behind you, or on the side of you. One of the things that I remember my mother saying to me when I got a little older was in reference to an old premonition that Miss Cora once told her: "This boy is going to die young because he knows too much."

My mother repeated that premonition for almost a week. She couldn't sleep, as a result, and she would wake up and come into my room to make sure I was breathing because old folks believed those premonitions. The truth was for some, they'd seen these premonitions come true.

Ma was petrified that Miss Cora had said that. This old premonition made me think back on a time when Ma said that I could fully form sentences and carry on conversations before I could even walk. From that point on, I've been able to effectively communicate my thoughts, which has helped me in both my personal and professional life. As a youngster riding the subway or city bus, I would read advertisement signs, street names, food labels, and anything that was in front of me.

I began to challenge the notion that I knew too much

by trying to learn as much as I possibly could. I believe that because I took the prospect of learning so seriously, it impacted those around me.

God's grace allowed me to rise above pitfalls but not without a few bumps and bruises along the way. On several occasions, I came extremely close to what could have derailed my life. Evidently lots of people were praying for me. As they say, it takes a village, and I do believe they were there to help and protect me. As a result, I was able to reason and think critically when it came to peer pressure. I had developed a mature sense of what I needed to do versus what I wanted to do. Living in Bed-Stuy was not easy. By the time I was eighteen, I personally knew of six young people, including an extended family member, who died tragically. The very traumatic way some were killed is forever etched in my mind.

The scary thing is that it became the status quo for these types of tragedies to occur. You could have been spending time with them one day, and the next day, you were faced with their funeral. As surreal as it was, the following day you were back on the stoop or project bench talking about the girls and what you were going to do next weekend. Even though you would miss them, their memory faded quickly.

For those of us who were still in the land of the living, we opted not to dwell on grief too long. I suppose that was a defense mechanism that helped us to move on and not get caught up in our feelings. Occasionally you might think about someone that may have perished in that struggle, but it was only for a fleeting moment, then back to the present. I know that may sound cold or unfeeling, but it was very tough to have endured that at such a young age. Even today I use that defense mechanism to shut out unpleasantness and call on *faith*.

I cannot always remember the exact dates these horrible things happened to friends or associates, but I usually recall the last conversations that I had with them. The surrealness of that is, I may have had a cool conversation with them one day and then the next day, they were gone. That reality was ironic and unreal. Unfortunately, this occurred too often in Bed-Stuy and the surrounding neighborhoods.

It didn't become real until it was at your doorstep, in the building next door to you, or your friend who lived in the apartment next to you for five or six years. Gone due to tragedy. The rest of us were constantly pressured to make something of ourselves by the adults.

CHAPTER 2

MOTHER'S GROWTH AND GRACE PLAN

"Courage is the most important of all the
virtues, because without courage you can't
practice any other virtue consistently. You
can practice any virtue erratically, but
nothing consistently without courage."

—*Maya Angelou, memoirist and poet*

BY THE TIME I was seven, I was a latchkey kid. Ma made sure I had the key to the house beneath my undershirt, where no one could see it. When school let out, Ma was at work, so I had to let myself in with the key. Being a latchkey kid, I didn't come home to Ma's cookies and milk waiting on the kitchen table. I had to unlock two deadbolts and three security-size padlocks to enter my house. Living in a tough but loving neighborhood, we were blessed to have people watching out. However, there were 'those people' who would stand on the corners and give you the "look" to try to intimidate you. But I wasn't one to be intimidated. I learned early on to look people dead in the eye and keep walking unless they addressed me by my name. The only way they could do that was if they knew me. One learned early to not stop for unnecessary conversations. You had to keep it moving while looking people in their eyes in case you had to remember a face.

When I flash back to that part of my life, I can remember my mother telling me certain things she expected of me; go to school, get good grades, and behave. "Remember, you are representing me and our entire family." I learned to cook, clean, and shop by the time I was twelve years old. I could master these tasks like any adult. Even today, I do grocery shopping, cooking, and cleaning. Once, I responded to her saying, "All this cooking and cleaning is girl's stuff." She responded, "Well, until we get a girl, you're going to do it!" And I did. My mother was the inspiration for it all. She was my teacher, my inspiration, and I'm a better person today because of her unrelenting dedication and direction.

Ma used to say, "I know I wasn't the best mother." She may not have exercised a lot of patience or tolerance for nonsense, but I thank God for her diligence and guardrails. I bumped against the guardrails like bumper cars, and they surely caused me bumps and bruises. My wife and family reap the benefits of those guardrails in my early life, as the structure made me a better person. Today, I'm a legitimately a good teammate to my wife. My wife will come in and cook after work, and I realize that she's tired after working hard all day, so I'll swoop into the kitchen to clean it up after she has prepared the meal. Sometimes we switch off playfully. I am a dynamic cook, cleaner and housekeeper, so it's no big deal to share my skills with my partner for life.

We lived in a three-story studio apartment over a dry cleaner in Bed-Stuy. My uncle owned a luncheonette in the neighborhood. Although there were Asian, Jewish, and Italian shop owners, there were also many prosperous Black entrepreneurs and shop owners. This gave me a sense of pride. It also gave a glimpse into the possibility of entrepreneurship. This was my first exposure to business, and it showed me why customers are so important. When I think about my beginning, hearing people make the declaration that I wouldn't live past twenty-one, or that I would either be on drugs, locked up, buried deep in the Evergreen cemetery, I have to thank God for a praying mother who sent me to church and was proactive in making sure I didn't get trapped in the tragedy because I almost bought into the lie.

My mother started sending me to church early on. She felt it offered a haven and an association of positive people that could help me stay grounded. No matter where we lived, I was required to get to church even if I had to take a bus across town. In the early days, we lived close to the church, so I walked there and since some of my good friends attended, I really didn't mind going.

My pastor always looked out for young people like me, and especially those who didn't have a dad in their home. I felt especially fortunate that I had the presence of my pastor as a role model. He inspired whole generations of people. In my urban upbringing directed by a single mother, I had all of the things that a normal suburban kid had. Cub Scouts, Boy Scouts, the marching band and the basketball league, baseball. My childhood friends and associates with similar backgrounds did not have access to this empowering environment even though we were in the same community. There is not enough said about supportive parents, positive role models and people that looked out for you. This village that helped raise me is responsible for the scouts, the basketball leagues, the uniforms, the registration fees and all that afforded me a life of opportunity and a divergent path from the self-destructive life so many of my friends headed to.

The village may seem overbearing to the youth, because they want to do what the other kids are doing. Ultimately, it will pan out and a fulfilling life can and will eventually be realized. As youth, all we can see are the barriers to the excitement and good times. Later, it will make sense, and you will be grateful not only for the oversight, but also, for the underlying love that carried it in the first place.

Around the age of seven, I was fortunate and favored to be working for my uncle. My job at first was filling the shelves at his luncheonette. Little did I know that would become my life's work, as I was fated to enter the world of retail. My uncle was especially focused and doting on me because he felt I was smart and had a bright future.

I can remember an unpleasant experience, not wanting to eat the lunch that was served to us at the grade school in Bed-Stuy. My mother was puzzled as to why I wouldn't eat the school lunch. I finally I told her that I refused to eat the school lunch because it was so terrible. Rather than take umbrage at my perceived stubbornness, she arranged for me to walk up the block to my uncle's place to eat lunch.

While the other kids were eating cold peanut butter sandwiches and split pea soup, I was eating a cheeseburger or a fish sandwich and fries, and having a nice "soda", as we called it. At the end of the week, my mother paid my uncle $5 or $6 for my lunch tab, but the cost of what I ate was way more than that. Little did my mother know I had started stocking the shelves of his little grocery section in his luncheonette in order to help take care of the bill.

Ma knew my bill was more than the small amount she was paying, but I felt empowered earning my keep and being able to help out. Those shelves contained powdered soap, bleach and canned beans, as well as a wide variety of goods. In those days, we would write the price on the items with a magic marker.

My uncle would always say, "Make sure that the labels are facing out, and Michael, be sure that they are all perfect. Make sure everything is really blocked up the way it should be." Meaning, arrange the detergent with the detergent, the beans with the beans, and so forth.

Those were my early days of learning merchandising and the importance of making things look good. The customers would come in and purchase goods and I replenished the stock and did display merchandising before I knew what those words meant. I watched my uncle treat his customers and the community with respect. Part of this conditioning was having a positive place for people to purchase their goods and services. He prided himself on maintaining a clean, well-stocked facility that made people proud to come in. As I reflect on my time working for him, my uncle taught me the basics of what I promote and expect from people today.

I know it's possible to treat a business, customers and community with dignity and respect. My uncle modeled that behavior to the utmost, which made him quite successful. When people know that you care, then they take care of you. Those lessons were ingrained in me early on as I watched and learned from my uncle as he operated his business. With lots of prayer warriors and a village watching over me, I had many opportunities as a young person to learn and grow, through my uncle's many successful business ventures.

I still think about an older neighbor, Miss Carter, "Granny Grit", as we called her. She might have been eighty years old, but she watched over me and other kids in the neighborhood like a hawk. In tandem, the ushers in the church made sure I behaved and would separate me and my friends if we got rowdy. In fact, I remember the kindness and nurturance coming through the sterned looks and when they would give you a tissue to spit candy out of your mouth during service. It had more to do with keeping order and teaching us to respect our surroundings. They all knew that we had boundaries, and they were empowered by our parents to take corrective action if needed. The village's mission in life was to make sure we stayed within those boundaries. Granny Grit heard my mother say, "Don't you go to that corner," so she made it a point to make sure I didn't go to that corner. Now, you can believe that I went to the corner, but I abstained from going *around* that corner because I knew that there was probably danger lurking. Also, I feared the risk of disappointing Ma and the corporal punishment that I would surely face.

The village was caring, supportive and noisy, all moving me forward to my destiny. My mother went to work to assure I had the things I needed to succeed in life. My village people knew she was hardworking. Therefore, a plethora of people lent a hand back in those days and I'm gratefully a product of those helping hands today.

There were other businesses in the community: a barbershop, news and candy stand, dry cleaner, and the Tu Ten bar. They were all within steps of our apartment.

The business owners were well-respected men who came into the community to serve and deliver. Some of them lived in the community as my uncle did. It was a feeling of pride to know that Mr. Fox and others, at that time, owned their buildings. I didn't come to know what ownership and wealth building felt like until later in life. But I did discover what a respected man looked like. In addition to running their businesses, they were respected community leaders, they helped people, and they gave credit to folks in times of need. Their actions and attitudes filled me with pride and a sense of purpose. I endeavored to model those same behaviors and principles as I looked ahead to taking care of my family and the people that meant so much to me.

"It takes a village to raise a child" is an African proverb, which means that an entire community of people must provide for and interact positively with children for those children to experience and grow in a safe and healthy environment.

CHAPTER 3

RACISM IS OVER

"We must accept finite disappointment,
but never lose infinite hope."

—*Martin Luther King, Jr., minister and
leader of the civil rights movement*

IN THE LATE 1960s, I was blessed to be bused to a predominantly Caucasian school in Ridgewood, New York. It was there that I learned the value of assimilation at a very early age. I came out of a primarily Black and Latino neighborhood, yet I had only two Black teachers in my life. The overwhelming majority of teachers I encountered were Caucasian and they were not living in my community.

In the fourth grade, I was bused out to the Ridgewood community to attend school, passing dozens of schools to satisfy the integration mandate. That first day, we were met with opposition. Ridgewood was an Italian-German neighborhood, and it was the first time I had ever felt racial tension other than what I saw on the TV.

While they never called us by any racial epithets, they did have a look of disgust. I remember hearing white students and parents yelling, "Go home, we don't want you here, we don't want our schools to turn bad" or things of that nature. This was the first time, to my knowledge, that I experienced any kind of racism. It was the first time I ever felt the sting of prejudice. Ironically on the second day of school, it was all gone. It was just like it had never happened. There were no police that I can recall. We arrived at school, were ushered off the bus, and we went into the school. Those next years were phenomenal.

By the time I was in the sixth grade and throughout that whole time I was in that public school, I was an *A* or *B* student. I was always considered a smart student. God had given me the wisdom of discernment. He had given me the discipline to do the work, the confidence to compete, and the wisdom to know that I was worthy to be there. By the time I was in the sixth grade, I was elected class president by my classmates who were predominantly white.

Back then, you would have sixth-grade classes from six-one thru six-eight. Those in classes six-one thru six-three were considered "bright". Then some kids had challenges as you went from six-four to six-eight. I was in the six-one class and served as the president of the entire sixth grade. It was so interesting that the eleven-year-old white girls, who were my age, were the ones that were lifting me up, campaigning for me and making signs. I don't remember guys as much as

I remember the young ladies lifting me and writing poster boards with my name on it. Rosemary and Cassandra were instrumental to my success.

Emboldened, I remember declaring to Aunt Dot, who's ninety years old now, "Racism is over!"

She replied, "Racism will never be over."

"No, that can't be possible. I was voted class president! Everyone supported me."

I was somewhat dumbfounded by my aunt's statement; however, I had to consider her upbringing in Georgia and Florida during the 40s and 50s. I never doubted what she said because I knew my aunt would never try and diminish my accomplishments. She's been in my corner since birth!

Aunt Dot loves tacos so I recently cooked them for her and my mother. Fifty years later, over that meal, we talked about how proud I was to have two white girls as my campaign managers. She said she mentioned racism because she wanted me to understand the realities of the world. This is the only time I remember anyone from my family saying anything about race.

I had a good friend, a German-Italian boy, in the sixth grade, who I used to have lunch with at his house. Inspiration comes from many areas. Stevie was a good friend and neither of us saw color. We would often leave school at lunch (even though school lunch was better in Queens, we still took that as a chance to expand our friendship). It's amazing how much fellowship you can foster around food. We received strange looks from the people who would see us walking in the neighborhood to his house for lunch.

His mother would invite me in to have lunch with him (that's when you could go off campus to eat). It was still safe for me at that point, even though many parts of New York and Brooklyn were racially segregated, and there could be potential danger if you were caught in the wrong neighborhood after a certain time of day. We were not exempt from it, but the grace of God protected and covered me. Racial discord was flaring up all over the country, but we did not see it exhibited around us. Through all those interactions, I was being better prepared for my later years in life. I know that there were people, places, families, kids, and adults that crossed my path at the right time in my life. They each left me with something. I hope I did the same for them.

That year, I had a wonderful teacher named Mrs. Honig, a Jewish woman from Rego Park, New York. She always gave me positive feedback and reinforcement, encouraging me to work hard and to continue to excel. She would also tell me when she didn't think I had done my best.

My journey in the late 60s allowed me to end up in a junior high school in that same neighborhood in Ridgewood, New York. We had moved to another part of Bed-Stuy and that proved interesting as well. At that time, we were zoned for specific schools. Junior high school was dynamite. I was a straight-A student. Every year, I was on the honor roll. Then high school came, and I ended up in a school that I didn't want to attend. It was Boys High in Bed-Stuy, affectionately called "The High". It was renowned for sports heroes, doctors, scholars, and lawyers in the '40s, '50s, and early '60s. By the time I arrived, The High was something different than what it had previously been celebrated for. That first year, I was petrified. The school was an all-boys prep school, and I was not at all used to some of the elements and guys that I had to encounter.

You quickly learned there were different groups of guys: the hustlers, the scammers, and the boosters. They were different yet they were all survivors. These were young men, most of whom were more mature than me. Some of them even had mustaches and beards in the ninth and tenth grade, which I didn't quite understand. They did everything, including selling drugs and other illegal street merchandise.

There was a negative element that was now swirling around in this great school that had graduated so many scholars, doctors, and sports heroes. Knowing what it was, and seeing it evolve into what it had become was overwhelming, disappointing and quite frightening because I now had to go to school there.

At that time, you could use a different address to enroll in the school of your choice. However, once new regulations were established, I had no choice but to attend The High. By the tenth grade, I had learned to adapt. This trait, adapting, has served me well in both my career and life.

Most of these guys, who had money and all the trappings of a hustler's life, became my friends. I experienced many highs and lows in my newfound relationships. I saw other youth being used and abused mentally and physically.

I believe my discernment was heightened because of being so involved with them daily. Through it all I was able to maintain respectable grades and keep my reputation intact, even though I took a few detours here and there. God's grace kept me from some of the infractions that many of my classmates dealt with. All too many of them have gone to jail, turned into drug addicts, or got left behind. I guess that is the simplest way I could say it, as life took its toll on everyone in that incendiary environment.

By the time I was an adult and building a life, I encountered a multitude of races, religions, sexual orientations, and political opinions. Those early years being exposed to differences in K-8th grade, Little League, summers in the south, and even staying weekends at my aunt and uncle's house in a predominantly Caucasian neighborhood taught me: tolerance, empathy, respect, perseverance, and confidence. As a result of my upbringing and exposure, we've lived in mostly non-diverse neighborhoods where we thrived because we were good neighbors, and we were blessed to have good neighbors. I had a chance to become part of the village where we touch each other's lives in a positive, impactful way. I cared for the communities we've lived, and I also received permission from parents to constructively address their children if I saw them participating in activities that would affect them personally— the goal always being to pour into children positive energy. I also hoped that the children and their parents remembered the Byrons as kind, thoughtful, and caring neighbors, and communal.

CHAPTER 4

ON THEIR SHOULDERS

"You are where you are today because you stand on somebody's shoulders. And wherever you are heading, you cannot get there by yourself. If you stand on the shoulders of others, you have a reciprocal responsibility to live your life so that others may stand on your shoulders. It's the quid pro quo of life. We exist temporarily through what we take, but we live forever through what we give."

—*Vernon Jordan, civil rights attorney*

BEING RESPECTFUL CAUSED people to gravitate to me. When it came to people who were different, I made a point to make them feel welcomed. It's been said, "You have to show yourself friendly in order to gain friends." In terms of *friends*, I can't say I have a lot of them, but I do have a lot of acquaintances and relationships. They were developed because of that early mindset and my willingness to be vulnerable and open to new things, new people, new ways, and ultimately, new foods.

By the time I was fifteen years old, because of developing a taste palette with my uncle, I had probably eaten dozens of types of cuisine. If he had a taste for that type of food, we would experience it in a restaurant or take-out.

My uncle introduced me to so many different cultures and experiences. We went to a Jewish deli to get pastrami sandwiches, and they were so delicious that even today, I can't find a Pastrami sandwich to rival it. I am so enriched today because of that socialization. Having a sense, an understanding of what is presently deemed *cultural competence*, led me to be able to embrace it in its fullness and be curious enough to want to know and learn more. Whatever relationships I would be in, professional, friends or sports, I could be effective. Food is the universal connector.

My pastor's conviction was not to see me lost to the system. He had a stronghold on me that I couldn't shake loose. He set up job opportunities at some nice places for me like A&S department store, Martin's department store, and the Brooklyn Public Library. These were outstanding, visible jobs that he created by leveraging his relationships in city government and retail establishments. Many people would ask for his help obtaining a job, and I never did—yet he would always find me one. He knew that productive work would keep me grounded and out of trouble. I went to those jobs even when I didn't want to go. I endured the stares of the people and them not wanting to be around me because it was an all-Caucasian environment in some of the department stores. They were thinking, *why are you here? Who did you know to get here?* You could just see the quizzical stares, and I was a discerning, young person, so I knew exactly what they were thinking, but my job was to let them know that I belonged.

In Lower East Side, with Jewish merchants running most of the business community, we would say phrases like "Jew it down" when it came to haggling prices. I learned to turn off all these skewed phrases, however; I didn't want to be the subject of someone else's discriminatory words either. Words matter! In retail, I knew I was representing the whole community. I had to be punctual and well-dressed. I had to be earnest when counting money and be courteous on the good-bye, seeing people out. I was fourteen years old and went on to work for the three largest department stores. Our pastor saw me as someone who could bring joy and service to the neighborhood.

I remember him saying, "I don't care what anyone says, or how they look at you. As long as they don't do anything immoral or illegal to you, you go to work. You do the work that you're supposed to do, and you do it with excellence. They'll soon figure out why you're there because you can do it as well as they can."

I always kept that with me. The pastor was always in my ear, checking up on me. He expected me to give back to the community as he was doing, and other young adults were doing. His impact pointed me in the right direction. To know I was always involved in a church made him feel accomplished. Once the pastor's wife told my mother that she had a vision of me speaking in front of thousands. From then on, she inquired about my wellbeing.

I was indebted to community center leaders and people who had known me over the years. We were living in the projects in Brooklyn, where there was an awesome community center, a positive place for the youth to gather. It was a fantastic resource. Everyone respected the leadership there. Both leaders of the community center worked other full-time jobs, but made sure from 5:00 p.m. to 9:00 p.m., we had access to the center. These leaders were both college graduates. They continuously engaged us in conversation about living a better life. They both had families and yet, they made sure that five nights a week, we had a place to play basketball, chess, and ping pong. I hung with a bunch of goofy people when I was a teenager, but I had a lot of people watching me. I didn't realize it until later in life when my mother told me the story of Miss Barbara, one of the two leaders.

I knew they cared because they spoke to me differently and I responded to them differently. I often think of Miss Barbara, who was a very attractive woman, maybe thirty-six or so. Everyone had a crush on her! We all thought we might have the opportunity to date her. I didn't know how or why we thought that, but nevertheless we did. I may have looked at her that way too, but I never engaged in the locker room banter about wanting to be with her.

I looked at Miss Barbara as an adult, someone who cared and sacrificed for us. She would come in at night and open the community center so we would have somewhere to be, as opposed to being on the street or in a dice game; somewhere where we shouldn't have been.

Before I saw her beauty, I saw the opportunity and kindness she offered. No one has to do that. Surely, she earned a salary from the City of New York, but she did her job unselfishly and with excellence. She dutifully had the place open for us so we could come in and socialize in the afternoon for a few hours.

My scout leaders were also influencers in my life. Deacon Gilchrist and Mr. West were strong men. One was a postal worker, and the other was a sanitation truck driver. They were Christians and I'm sure they had their own struggles in life. By the time I encountered them, they were in their forties and fifties, and they both had families. I can tell you that they would administer some corporal punishment if they had to, and they had permission from our parents to do so.

I didn't receive any of that corporal punishment. In fact, the worst I ever received was an ear pulled or a headlock. That would be about all I needed to get me back in line. They never overstepped their bounds and did what they did out of love. There was never any malice in their hearts. These men were considerate and were role models as well. When you see a man who picks up trash with his hands being moved up to driving the truck, and you see him leave his house every morning with the *New York Daily* news under his arms wearing a suit as he goes to pick up trash, it gives you a sense of pride and hope.

I never saw the job they did as negative or demeaning.

Both men owned their brownstones and had tenants, all on their public service wages. They lived a middle-class lifestyle and displayed the possibility of being successful. To see them in suits made me want to be a successful businessman. I often read *Ebony* magazine and would fix my eyes on the well-dressed men in the pages that looked like me. To see gentlemen from my own neighborhood dressed that way gave me vision of a better life.

As Dr. King said, "If you're a street sweeper, be the best one you can be." Be on time, do what you say you're going to do, and be a man of your word. A phrase I remember from that time is "Your word is your bond." I heard that a lot from men in the community who were older than me. So, it always stuck with me. All those little subliminal messages, interactions, guidance, and the guardrails that I can completely see now, I didn't always see the value of as I was growing up. I thank God for the lessons learned and feel it my responsibility to share them with the coming generations and anyone willing to listen.

It is clear that there was always somebody pouring into me. Out of the crowd of adults and people I knew, there was always someone encouraging me to stay in school, investing in Michael Byron. I know I didn't thank them at the time, but I am truly grateful they took the time to invest in me whether up close or from afar. I wasn't mature enough to have known that then. As my grandmother uses to say, "If you live long enough…you'll learn some things." Well, I've been blessed with a full life having met, worked alongside, been hurt by, broke bread with, celebrated wins and losses, and received advocacy, mentoring, feedback, from so many good (and not-so-good) people. Through it all, I'm still standing. *The Grace Effect*!

CHAPTER 5

ANCHORING YEARS OF JOY AND SORROW

"Trust yourself. Create the kind of self that you
will be happy to live with all your life. Make the
most of yourself by fanning the tiny, inner sparks
of possibility into flames of achievement."

—*Golda Meir, Israel's first and only female head
of government and first in the Middle East*

A FEW MONTHS after turning nineteen years old, I realized I needed to make the decision to leave New York in order to have a chance and experience life on my own. Therefore, with my mother's guidance and blessing I went to live with my father in Florida. I had initially connected with my father around the age of seven. He lived in Florida, where me and my cousins would go for summer vacations.

That's another part of my early childhood. We would

vacation in Florida from the time I was seven until about age fourteen. As soon as school ended in New York, we would head to Florida where we had a whole host of friends and relatives to enjoy the summer with. My grandmother, Jannie, took care of us, providing three meals a day, washing our clothes and watching over us. My grandmother wasn't the doting type, however; she exhibited her love and affection through the special care we received for eight weeks in the summer. My grandmother would rise before the sun rose to pick peas or strawberries and prior to her departure, she would cook us a big breakfast and leave it on top of the stove or in the oven. My grandmother was my protector. If my mother would chastise me for something, Grandma would always defend me, and that was an incredible feeling that never left. I concur with Maya Angelou: "I've learned that people will forget what you said, people will forget what you did, but people will never forget how you made them feel."

We had a fun time riding bikes for miles and being outside without fear or harm coming to us. Those eight weeks in the summer, living with my grandmother, doing chores, and being with my cousins was more fun than you could ever imagine. It was sort of apropos that I returned to Florida after my grandmother passed away to start adulthood. The memories we created were a testimony to freedom and excitement. Those summers were a blessing and at the end of the vacation, we would often cry knowing that soon we had to return to the "ghetto" (or as we remembered it as, "talkin bout the ghetto", singing with Donny Hathaway). In Florida alongside my cousins, I learned respect for family, homestead, and the value of relaxed boundaries that were fully enforced in Brooklyn.

When I arrived in Florida to live with my father, I quickly discovered that me and him were on different continents regarding our expectations of each other. I expected him to open the checkbook and buy me a car and other things to make up for lost time. What he didn't realize was that I was an adult and had been working and paying my way from a very early age. I possessed a self-sufficient mindset and survival tactics honed from a very early age.

I had a lot of money that I'd saved up from various jobs in New York, in addition to working a nine-to-five. I didn't really need him to support me financially, but I did need him to get my bearings straight before I could start to venture out on my own. I decided to adhere to his rules, however, that was short lived. Dad had a small catering business that me and my half-brothers helped to operate. Our responsibilities included catering weddings and parties on the weekends. I learned how to decorate cakes, shoot photography, cater full meals, arrange flowers, bake pies, and cook a variety of foods from my father. I also had a chance to learn from and enjoy the presence of my dad's family: aunts, uncles, siblings, and grandparents, who were entrepreneurs and community organizers serving their country, and were so much of who I've become personally and professionally. They are all residents of heaven now, and because they lived, I have endured. Because they lived, I have been a beneficiary, and so has my child. Her children will also.

My father had been a baker in the U.S. Navy and now had his own barbeque restaurant that served a variety of items including burgers and other fast foods. My dad was a hustler and always talked about multiple revenue streams just like my uncle in New York. He would also load his old station wagon and go to the neighboring town to sell rib sandwiches and whole pies every weekend. I got the chance to learn a lot about running a restaurant from him, but he expected that we would work so many hours a day that it challenged me and caused me to not consider staying in business with him. I had other ideas about utilizing my time and earning my worth. Interestingly, both my uncle and father would use their business to control my time. I don't believe they meant to cause harm, but they grew up at a time you were not allowed to become complacent, and there was no time for rest. I don't remember either of them taking extended vacations.

I was going to college and between school and working a full-time job, plus working with him, I was exhausted most of the time. He didn't want to see the image of me at nineteen years old merely sitting around with my feet on an ottoman. He thought as soon as you came home from school, you should start working—cutting wood for the barbeque pit, baking pies or making cake icing. We had fundamental differences when it came to issues like that. But just a few months later, when I turned twenty, I decided to move out of my dad's house and get my own apartment. I continued to work, go to school, and I was having a great time learning, exploring, and getting back to the time where I wanted to learn and achieve as many things as I possibly could.

I started working in a small independent retail grocery store as a stocker and cashier while going to school. I was still working on the weekends to help my father and working in a men's clothing store in other hours I could squeeze in. After a while I took a break from school, and it wasn't until later in life that I went back and completed my college degree. I did so because I felt it was important to be able to present a positive example for my future child to emulate.

Before the birth of my daughter and prior to my marriage, I spent a lot of time involved with church. I had many friends both in and out of church, and we experienced different things than I had experienced in New York. Things that relate to women, dating, travel and the like. I often thought about my father, wondering if I were wasting time and spending energy on things that were not important, courtesy of his influence. However, like everything there are life lessons and roads we must travel due to our decisions. I grew from the experiences, the confusion of it all. You see, when you are first on your own, you really don't have any set structure or guidelines. When I was still living at home with my mother, I had a definite set of structures and boundaries. I knew when, what, and how because my mother and the village established the parameters. I knew what I could do, and what I could not do. Now that I was an adult, I had to manage and maintain everything and work through becoming an adult.

By the time I was twenty-one, I had joined a local church there in Florida. I was so dedicated that the day after I was in a car accident, I was in church. I honestly felt like something was missing in my life and I knew it was God at that point. The Lord covered me through that accident and continues to do so to this day. The actual accident wasn't anything devastating or horrible; I rolled the car I was driving and was able to get out and walk. I didn't hurt anyone or myself. It was a rainy night, I was somewhere where I shouldn't have been, and I ended up losing control of the car. I still remember every minute of the accident as if it happened yesterday. It's funny how things can end up exactly where they should be even if you are trying your best to go in another direction.

I made up my mind that I was going to start attending church and coincidentally, it ended up being the same church that my mother went to as a youth. In fact, my grandfather helped to build the church. His name is still on the building. I became a member of the church and sang in the choir and did the things that I remember the young adults doing for us back in Bed-Stuy. I went into a mode of operation focused on keeping myself on the straight and narrow. Through it all, I maintained a job, continued going to school and progressed in my career as I experienced various opportunities and options.

If I could fast forward, I would say the early 80s is when my life took an interesting turn. I had lost my focus and direction living in Florida. It wasn't fast enough for me, and I felt like I was losing my "New York swagger". I hadn't finished school and worked the multiple jobs. I loved my life but was growing restless and missing Brooklyn. The excitement of Manhattan, Brooklyn and the Bronx was missing. The Sunshine State felt rather sluggish. So, I moved back to New York in the early 80s for one year.

Arriving back home after living in Florida in the mid- to late 70s, I found that New York had changed tremendously. It had been five or six years since I had last lived in Brooklyn. I almost didn't recognize the place, and I had trouble recognizing some of my immediate family not because of the outward appearance but rather, their demeanor. You know time has a way of changing you, and the adage "you can always go home" didn't seem plausible.

I had seven first cousins whom I loved dearly. While I was in New York for that year, one of my cousins was murdered in a robbery in the family business. It devasted me, and vengeance filled my heart. During my youth, it was commonplace to avenge anyone who violated you or yours. Remember, I talked about leaving New York because of the streets, and now, the streets landed at my doorstep. During my sabbatical back to the city, I worked for my uncle part-time during the day and had a full-time position at a retail bakery at night.

I still remember getting off work and going to my aunt's house in Queens. This was my cousin's mother. I would stop by the house every mid-morning to check in and visit. That day, we received a call from someone in Brooklyn informing us that my cousin had been shot in a robbery.

We all jumped in a car, including my aunt who had just gotten home, and headed into Brooklyn. The worst thing you could imagine had happened; my cousin was shot and died on the way to the hospital. I was thinking this was the worst decision I could have ever made to come back to New York.

A childhood friend had been killed in the street life early on and it still impacted me. That was the wakeup call that caused me to move to Florida in the first place, as well as needing my independence and being ready to stretch my wings and fly. Yet here it was happening all over again and landing at my doorstep. We were always told, "You won't make it to twenty-one."

We arrived at Kings County Hospital, one of the biggest hospitals in the Bed-Stuy section of Brooklyn. We went into the emergency room and started asking questions. My aunt was upset, as you can imagine. We asked for my cousin by name and the desk clerk said he could be in any of the triage rooms. God led me to the exact room where my cousin was lying with a sheet covering his body. I immediately recognized him due to his chewed fingernails. I knew him that well, we were like brothers, and I had no doubt that it was him lying there deceased on that gurney.

I still talk about it today, all these years later it's etched in my mind. I think God led me there because it would reshape my mind and heart toward how I needed to live my life. In fact, that previous November we were at the family home for Thanksgiving and my cousin who was tragically killed said to me, "Michael, you need to go back to Florida. Your life is there, you're too smart to be here and you don't need to keep working in the family business." I thought he was trying to keep me from being a part of the family business.

The truth is, it was his way of looking out for me because he was well-aware of what Bed-Stuy, Brooklyn and New York had become in the 80s. I was in a place that was more volatile than when I left it in the late 70s. He was trying to keep me from that element and the danger that had begun to seep into the fabric and ultimately our family. I didn't realize what he was trying to tell me until after he was gone. I thank God that he used my cousin, even in his darkest hours, to tell me right from wrong.

Only my cousin could do that because he could do no wrong in my eyes. As we grew up, he was the person I looked up to and admired tremendously.

He taught me how to dress, how to talk to women, and ultimately how to become a young man. He taught me many different things that were life lessons, and I still utilize them to this day. I will never forget the gift he gave me. Insight and influence. His insight helped to forge my life moving forward. His influence translated a scared, struggling, little kid into a young man capable of dealing with the streets and the complete world that loomed in front of me.

His death was very traumatic for me, and consequently that fall, I went back to Florida because my future wife and the girl I selfishly left behind came to rescue me. This was God telling me, "Here is your 'Ram in the Bush' once more—you need to take hold and listen to the messages from those who love and have invested in you." *The Grace Effect!*

She was ultimately the motivating factor, along with my cousin, that convinced me to move back to Florida. My life began to find purpose and direction again. I began to see a renewed spirit and detachment from a place that caused me so much pain at young age. Everything that I had, a strong mother, the benefits of church structure, the village that raised me, my cousin's vision, and the relationship with my future wife, all culminated in that place and time. I was in a dark place, yet God shed light on my situation and presented my soon-to-be-wife, my rescuer, to me. I think of Psalms 91, 11-12: *For he shall give his angels charge over thee, To keep thee in all thy ways. They shall bear up thee in their hands, Lest thou dash thy foot against a stone.*

One of the primary reasons I moved back to Florida was to attend her sister's wedding. Initially I was only supposed to attend the wedding, but eventually I became her escort. After participating in that wedding, I realized that she was to be my wife. I made up my mind that the New York chapter of my life was over. I stayed in Florida and my life improved for the better. I began to mature as a person, marriage was in the works, and I couldn't have been more excited.

The next four years were filled with myriad activities. I continued to work fulltime and concentrated on completing my college degree. The most enjoyable portion of that was spending time with my future wife. We were inseparable and were soon making plans to settle down together. We married in 1984, and recently celebrated forty years of wedded bliss. She has been my rock in a weary land and my north star as we have traveled this journey together.

A few short years later, God blessed us with a baby girl that changed my life forever. All the lessons my mother and the rest of village instilled in me are the tools I needed to rely on to be entrusted with my wife and baby girl's lives.

Being grounded in church, family, and love helped me to appreciate the decision to remain in Florida. By now, I was married, and we had our daughter who was only six months old. Life was normal, my wife and I were moving in our respective careers and enjoying being married. We also joined an awesome church. (My wife had been raised as a Methodist, and I was a Baptist. She decided to join a Baptist church we had found in our new town so we would raise our daughter under one faith.)

While all was going great for us, another story of tragedy was unfolding in Brooklyn. Five years after losing my cousin, my uncle whom I looked up to, my role model, and the father of the cousin I lost, passed away from illness, suffering from the unbearable grief of losing his firstborn in such a tragic way in a place that should've been our sanctuary and breeding space for success. There I was heading to another funeral and a loss that felt insurmountable, and the one thing I thought about at that time was being there for the rest of the family.

Two years after his funeral, I received a call that my other cousin was missing. This was the brother of my cousin that had been killed earlier in the 80s. I took off work for a week to see if I could help locate him. I went back to New York and searched tirelessly for him, only to be notified by the police almost a week after I arrived that they had found his body. They requested that a family member come and identify the body. I volunteered, along with my uncle, my mother's brother. Police vehicles were surrounding the ambulance. I stepped into the ambulance and right away recognized him due to his fingers, (just as I had been able to identify his brother's body). I think this cousin delivered a different message.

He had an entrepreneurial spirit and could have been whatever his heart desired; however, decisions caused him to take a different path that impacts our family and me personally still all these years later. Four years earlier, he had been the best man at my wedding. Years before his death, he had given me similar advice as his brother had. "Michael, you are a smart man. This is not the life for you. You should stay in Florida, and don't get caught in this life." They both left me with powerful messages, and ironically, God used these tragedies to help shape and inspire me to live a better life. I had been the first one in the family to see their bodies after they were discovered.

I realize one would have been seventy-two, the other, sixty-six. I dream of the conversations we would have today amidst so much laughter. We were raised together. Those losses were tremendous. They saw something in me throughout our lives and continued to reiterate it. One year later, another first cousin died, my mother's brother's son. We were not as close; however, his death left me feeling survivor's remorse. We all were cut from the same cloth, bloodline, and potential to live full lives. These cousins had two parents and access to whatever they wanted, unlike me. As a family, losing four men in the 1980s was devastating, and left a void in our lives forever.

God has used me to console, care for, and love their remaining family and to be a light for current and future generations. I pray God will continue to keep me in good health, faith driven, and pursuing a purposeful life, so that I may continue to build a foundation, make an impact, and "Spread Love the Brooklyn Way"!

CHAPTER 6

RELATIONSHIP ROADMAP

"The Kingdom is the love of God prevailing in
politics, in business, in government, in media.
It is all the impact of the laws of God creating a
social environment where the strong help the weak,
where those who have give to those who don't. It's
a society where relationships are built on love."

—*Myles Munroe, minister and motivational speaker*

EARLY EXPERIENCES AND life lessons prepare you for the multitude of relationships, colleagues, friends and people that God places in your life at the exact time for a variety of reasons.

I grew in Mt. Carmel Baptist Church in Bed-Stuy, where the movie "Do The Right Thing" was filmed, and coincidently, my family started our lives in a church with that same name in Florida. I am reminded of Romans 8:28: *And we know that for those who love God all things work together for good, for those who are called according to his purpose.* The Grace Effect. In that church, I had many conversations about my career since my wife and daughter were my primary world, and there was a lot of movement or requests for relocations during that time period.

One of the first supervisors I had the pleasure of working with managed people through trust and a teamwork philosophy. I thrived under his leadership and felt his concern when he stood up for me the moment an individual hurled a racial epithet towards me in a retail environment. In that same environment, I met a young man from Boston who became a champion, and because of him, my career flourished for three decades. We're still friends today, and in 2023, he and his lovely wife attended my daughter's wedding.

For one of my first promotions, I was instructed to pack up and move my family to a different location in the state we lived in. I spoke up for myself and shared our recent purchase of a home, my wife's career, my daughter just entering pre-school. The issue arose because the leadership wanted another person moving from out of state to become the district manager in the area I had cultivated and trained the staff in. Well, as God would have it, another longtime relationship stood in the gap and the decision was made to promote me to the location I had earned.

Relationships reign. Another supervisor, who has been a lifelong friend, was instrumental in my promotion to California. He arrived in Florida from the Northwest part of the country. He and his lovely wife treated me and my district peers like family and would open their home to us when we were opening or remodeling stores in the area they lived. I remember home-cooked meals and desserts, our own rooms in his fabulous home, love, care, and intentionality to break down any barriers that would impede our collective success was always apparent.

I set off on a journey to California that took me three and a half days to drive, and thoughts of leaving my family saddened me; however, my peers and I had always discussed getting the call from corporate. It was part of the ultimate journey that took me from Brooklyn to Florida, to California, to Boise and beyond. Along the way, I encountered people, places, and situations that helped mold and mature me. All these encounters took me back to a time I was elected class president, and God uses and placed people in my life for a reason and season. In many cases, some of those folks are still in my life, and have been a constant reminder of God's grace and path he set forth for me and those individuals.

When I think of how opportunities have presented them-selves over time, especially in my career and health of my family, they've always arrived at the time they were supposed to happen. I'm able to make that statement because I claimed and spoke those opportunities into existence. I believe you must see yourself and your dreams manifest deep into your soul. However, know the desires of your heart may not arrive when you feel them but rather, when God believes you're equipped to handle what you've requested. When you have done all you know and need to do, it is just standing in faith and allowing it to happen. You must believe in the possibility of possibilities. Often, God may hold a blessing because it might not be right for you or the right people haven't been placed in position so that you can fulfill your dream.

At each juncture, my wife was semi-prepared because we had discussed the career trajectory, I saw for myself, and the life I wanted for our family. She rolled with all the moves. However, when we moved to California, that was probably the most difficult because we were leaving family, friends, church, our network. God prepares you for the journey; you just have to be courageous enough to follow His path for your life. I remember the excitement and sadness having to leave my family, but I trusted God's direction and my ability to move forward and headed to Northern California.

I drove thousands of miles in a single day trying to get to my destination. When I arrived in Lafayette, Louisiana, I wanted to turn around. I thought I had made a huge mistake, but God quickly reminded me this assignment was what I spoke into existence years before, and He merely was opening the door to my future. I spent the night in Lafayette and headed out the next morning for my next stop in El Paso, Texas. When I arrived in El Paso for the night, I realized how large the state of Texas really was. I still remember the town of Lufkin, before El Paso, where I pulled over for gas and to stretch my legs. The gas station was straight out of the 1950s; it appeared that way because the pumps were old and there was a greasy spoon café attached to it. You had to pay for your gas purchase inside, so I went in to pay and walked into a place where I thought there was going to be trouble. What I had forgotten for a few seconds was God was with me as always. The folks looked at me, questioning my existence in this place. The clerk slammed my change down on the counter. I picked it up and was on my way. It's a wonder what you can process in merely a few seconds—tolerance, God speaking to me and having my back.

I looked in my rearview for at least twenty miles down the road. I woke up the next morning and drove from El Paso to Bakersfield, California, and the next morning, on into Sacramento, which was my destination.

Remember, I spoke about speaking things into existence. You also must be prepared for what you ask for. This assignment wasn't ideal; it was a broken division of the company I worked for, and the division was among the worst operationally in the entire company. I remember walking into my office where the person I was replacing had a marlin mounted on the wall. It was removed, but the smell was unbearable. The office needed to be cleaned and painted. The first call I received was from a supervisor saying I needed to visit stores and someone would come by the office to take me out to the field. I had numerous colleagues who were promoted like me and traveled thousands of miles to the new assignment, but didn't receive a sketchy reception like mine. I knew I was going to need The Grace Effect in this situation. I had traveled too far and waited for this opportunity, and there was no turning back.

I arrived on a Thursday, and that Sunday, I sought out a church to attend. I remember stopping at a Hispanic church and asking directions to the nearest Black Baptist church. They pointed me to a church that was located just down the street about a mile and a half from the hotel I was living in and near one of the stores I would be responsible for.

I entered that church and sat on the pew. A young woman sat next to me for a moment, then said "good morning" with a beautiful smile. "Is this your first time here?"

I said, "Yes, I just arrived in Sacramento on Thursday."

She beamed, "And you found the church already?"

Our conversation continued for a while, and at that moment, I realized how fortunate and favored I was. Here I was halfway across the country in a place I'd never been, yet I was having a pleasant conversation with a stranger. Little did I know this stranger would become one of the many good friends and an extension to my family that I would meet on my journey from Brooklyn to Boise.

I woke up that Sunday morning so grateful for a safe trip, promotion, and realizing how hard I had worked for this opportunity and how I was going to make a home for my family. As God had planned it, the young lady on the pew and her then fiancé whom I now call my brother and sister gave me their contact information and told me if I needed anything to give them a call. I didn't feel any trepidation or uneasiness in sharing my contact information as I normally would have, given my cloistered upbringing in Brooklyn. I felt at peace with my new friends, and we've experienced what seems like a lifetime together. The Grace Effect!

I arrived that October, and in November, we were celebrating Thanksgiving dinner with the parents of the young lady I had met at church. That shows you how God inadvertently places people in your life. When I think back over my journey there have been quite a few relationships that turned into lifelong friendship and extended family. This is how The Grace Effect manifested; I was having a tough week with my new assignment in California and missed my family, and my colleague and his loving wife invited me to their home for dinner. The invite was for 6:30 p.m., and I left their house at nearly 11:30 p.m. I overstayed my welcome, but I believe they felt my longing for family. The moments matter. I was enjoying the family environment and their children; one of the little girls was infatuated with the tassel on my shoes. The kids (young adults) have their owns families now. The menu was simple; however, it was their love, care, and a willingness to share with me that remains in my heart all these years later.

At the church we attended, we were assigned a family deacon, and we were fortunate to have a wonderful, retired military gentleman, who was like a phenomenal uncle or godfather. He was there for us spiritually and made sure we became active in the church, and that we exposed our daughter to all the church had to offer. We thrived and became part of the body, and ultimately had to leave due to another promotion. Another colleague took me under his wing. We both left big cities (Chicago and New York) in the pursuit of happiness, career and prosperity. He was wise beyond his years, and a devout family man with a few cool hobbies (travel, motorcycles, knives, and stocks). Needless to say, we have been investing in the market for a long time because of his knowledge and insight.

Brian A. Chalker said it best: "People always come into your life for a reason, a season and a lifetime. When you figure out which it is, you know exactly what to do."

CHAPTER 7

NEVER ENOUGH HEART

"The heart is great; indeed, it is through the heart
that come the great inspirations of life. I would a
hundred times rather have a little heart and no brain,
than be all brains and no heart. Life is possible,
progress is possible for him who has heart, but he
who has no heart and only brains dies of dryness."

—Swami Vivekananda, monk and philosopher

ON ONE OCCASION, after opening a brand-new store, then celebrating with a couple of libations, a senior executive said, "Michael, you are great at what you do and have a bright future with the company, but you think too much with your heart." I resented that because my mother always told me I had a big heart. I didn't think differently of him, but I wasn't going to take that advice. Instead, I chose to embrace the very essence of who I was—a person driven by passion, empathy, and an unwavering belief in the power of connection.

As I stood there, feeling the warmth of the room and the camaraderie that filled the air, I couldn't help but reflect on the countless moments that had shaped me. My mother's words echoed in my mind, reminding me that my heart was not a weakness but a strength. It had guided me through challenges, inspired me to build relationships, and ignited a deep-seated desire to uplift those around me. I remembered the late nights spent dreaming about this very moment, the opening of a store that wasn't just a business but a community hub—a place where people could come together, share their stories, and find solace in the simple act of shopping.

In that moment, I made a silent vow to remain true to myself, to let my heart lead the way, and to focus on what mattered most: the people who filled the aisles of the store, the employees who worked tirelessly to create a welcoming environment, and the customers who walked through the doors with hopes and expectations. I believed that by leading with empathy, I could foster a culture that valued genuine connections and mutual support.

I would continue to pour my heart into my work, to inspire others to do the same, and to create a legacy built on kindness, courage, and resilience. After all, in a world that often felt cold and transactional, I knew that the warmth of a big heart could light the way for many.

His words lingered in the air, and for a moment, I felt the weight of his expectations pressing down on me. But deep inside, I knew that my heart was my greatest asset, not a hindrance. It had guided me through countless encounters, allowing me to connect with customers on a deeper level, to sense their needs even before they articulated them. My mother's voice echoed in my mind, reminding me that empathy and compassion were not just traits to be admired but essential tools for success in any endeavor.

"Why can't I use both?" I echoed to myself, and realized this was my choice and I was going to follow my heart. I believed that intuition and intellect could coexist harmoniously; they were not opposing forces but rather, complementary aspects of a well-rounded individual. I could be analytical and strategic while also being kind and approachable.

This realization became a cornerstone of my philosophy in the workplace and in my personal life. I made it my mission to cultivate an environment where vulnerability and authenticity were celebrated rather than stifled. I initiated team building and encouraged open dialogue, where everyone could express their thoughts and feelings without the fear of judgment. I wanted to create a culture that valued emotional intelligence just as much as technical skills, understanding that the relationships we build with one another ultimately drive our collective success. As I navigated through my career, I encountered various leaders who embodied different approaches. Some were ruthless, climbing the corporate ladder by stepping on others, while others were compassionate, fostering a sense of community that inspired loyalty and dedication. I took notes from both, but the latter resonated with me profoundly. I wanted to be the kind of leader who uplifted others, who recognized their contributions, and who made them feel seen and valued.

In moments of doubt, I would reflect on my mother's

teachings. She often spoke of the concept of "servant leadership", a principle that emphasizes the importance of serving others first before seeking to lead. It was a powerful reminder that true leadership is rooted in humility and a genuine desire to make a positive impact. I strived to embody this philosophy in every interaction, whether it was with a colleague struggling under the weight of a project or a customer seeking assistance. I also learned that being authentic meant being vulnerable. It wasn't always easy; there were times when I felt the urge to put on a tough façade, especially in high-stakes situations. But I discovered that when I allowed myself to be open and honest about my struggles, it created a space for others to do the same. We bonded over our shared business challenges and family issues only to transform these moments of weakness into opportunities for growth and understanding.

As I continued to move up in my career, I became increasingly aware of the responsibility that came with my position. I was not just there to drive profits or meet targets; I was there to shape the culture of my team and by extension, the organization. I sought to lead by example, demonstrating that it was possible to be both successful and compassionate, ambitious yet grounded. I also made it a point to mentor younger professionals, sharing my experiences and encouraging them to embrace their true selves. I wanted to instill in them the same values my mother had imparted to me: the importance of kindness, integrity, and the courage to be vulnerable. I believed that by nurturing their authentic selves, they would not only excel in their careers but also, contribute positively to the workplaces they would inhabit.

In the end, it was this intertwining of heart and mind that defined my journey. I learned that success wasn't solely measured by titles or salaries but by the impact we had on those around us. As I reflected on my path, I felt a deep sense of gratitude for the lessons learned, the people met, and the moments that shaped me. I had come to understand that it was okay to feel deeply, to care passionately, and to lead with both heart and head. And so, I continued to navigate the intricacies of my professional and personal life, armed with the wisdom of my past and the hope for a future where authenticity and compassion would reign supreme.

CHAPTER 8

THE LEADER'S MIRROR

"Let us not look back in anger, nor forward
in fear, but around in awareness."

—James Thurber, cartoonist and playwright

WHEN I THINK back to my church upbringing and how the pastor, staff and volunteers sacrificed and helped create an environment for my safety, success and sense of well-being, I am humbled. You have a responsibility because once you get to a place—and I don't care where you are in life—you must do for others. I believe Dr. King said, "Life's most urgent and persistent question is what are you doing for others?" He's a fraternity brother of mine and I live by that mantra. My email signature underscored these words for the longest time, and they frame my world.

You must anchor your daily life on something that resonates with you, it helps develop your purpose and positive results. All the while, people will observe, scrutinize you with a certain sense of expectation (and that could be good or bad), taking in every move because as you elevate in the organization, the target on your back gets bigger and bigger.

When you move from a task-oriented role to an influential one, your level of engagement shifts. Your words and actions are important to accomplishing results. Interpersonal skills, communication and genuine caring are the required attributes for forming and fulfilling purpose.

I think one expectation would be to seek a certain degree of peace over your life as well. That peace incorporates your family, friends, community, and any situation you're associated with. There's an ability to communicate and get things done, there's a way that you become a person who can settle things, be a voice of reason. In corporate America it's tough, you're going to come up against a lot of people, but the gift of discernment comes to mind for me as well. If you pray about acquiring the gift of discernment, you begin to understand why it's truly a gift from God because it allows you to read and connect with people.

That gift of discernment, that vulnerability and to a certain degree, transparency, is something that you will need in every aspect of your life. People will inevitably be willing to open up to you more than they would if they didn't know you. People want to get to know you a little bit. Otherwise, people will make up in their own minds the narrative of your life, and it may be skewed or misguided. You don't have to tell your whole life story; however, people need to know enough to know who they are dealing with and what you stand for.

A great example is when I would move into a new neighborhood. I would normally go out of my way to introduce myself and waylay any concerns that I may be a nefarious individual. In that my position allowed me to drive a nice car, wear nice clothes and purchase a great house, I didn't want them speculating that I was a bad or indifferent element. In many cases, we were the first minority family to move into the neighborhood. When a few neighbors got to know us, our experience became not only more palatable but enjoyable, and we developed lifelong friendships.

Those relationships would have been hard to establish if we hadn't set those types of expectations for ourselves nor interacted proactively with others. This made them feel comfortable knowing we had similar values as everyone else in the neighborhood. I wanted them to know that I could replace the hinge on the front door or keep up my property while engaging a good neighbor.

I'd make sure that those initial individuals would spread my story and the message of positivity regarding Michael Byron. By controlling the narrative, people wouldn't need to peek through their venetian blinds and try to figure out who I am. Now, when I'm cutting the grass, folks shouldn't be reluctant to say "hello, hope you're having a nice day" because I've afforded them the ability to do so by controlling the narrative.

You must own some of the responsibility to show yourself friendly. By doing so, you can gain friends and expand your intentional ecosystem. I believe you're able to travel the path that God has outlined if you set high expectations for yourself. Mine has been to have a healthy, giving, serving, loving, and well-rounded life.

Without expecting to arrive at your prescribed destination, you can easily set yourself up for derailment. It's all about taking those life lessons, imparting them to others, whether family, friends, acquaintances, or colleagues. We have a responsibility to impart the wisdom we've learned and never sit in silence in a room where there are others.

I recently had a conversation with my nineteen-year-old niece who spent a year away in college and wanted to return home because of her insecurities and lack of exposure beyond the small town she was raised in. The village and parents encouraged her to return and complete her studies because it's the power source to freedom, and will build the confidence to follow the life God has designed for her. You see, I was one of the senior leaders responsible for recruitment at the university my niece was attending. Knowing she was somewhat of an introvert and insecure, I was planning to use my role to help her connect.

One of the reasons I took on that role was to help my company recruit talented minority students and to be an advocate for my niece in her new collegiate environment. I knew that some of my work probably would've benefited her while she was attending school. However, what I didn't realize was the impact my visit had on her and many other students on campus. Today, I'm proud to say my niece is a college graduate and a thriving young adult, and she's a role model for her younger sister, who is also pursuing her formal education. There were many expectations placed on me as one of the few only males of my generation in my immediate family still alive. With that heightened sense of expectation, many family members and friends saw me as a leader and an elder. It's as if they expected me to shoulder a leadership role to help shepherd other aspiring family members toward the road to success. I have accepted the challenge because I choose to uphold the tenets of Philippians 2:4, "Let each of you look not only to his own interests, but also to the interests of others."

The expectation of being a beacon of light for your family and friends is the greatest reward life can afford you. To have lived life long enough to be seen as that light exemplifies God's grace and favor. Ultimately, your accolades, degrees, certificates, awards and other things you've accomplished will be spotlighted in one vehicle or another; however, what matters most is how you lived your life, and how many lives were impacted and able to find their way because of your light.

There were many expectations I had for myself, like the ability to grow and have a career, accomplish wealth, accolades, and have a family. It was not just for self-preservation, there is generational preservation at stake. I remember my mother telling me "a closed hand cannot receive". To be a Sower of seed, a man must first open his hand before he can reap. God won't be able to bless you unless you open your hands and be generous. Being there for your family is not solely about the things you can give them although at times, it's a requirement.

Ultimately, it's about giving your time, attention, and sharing experiences that will help to guide others to succeed in whatever they are facing at the time they request your support. It may be taxing at times, yet my mother who is eighty-eight years old still gives her time and ear to family and church members who need an ear, ride to church, prayer or a shoulder to lean on. So many of my mother's generation are at different stages in their lives and as a result, don't have the peace in their lives for various reasons. Some in her generation are still working to support their family members because of decisions, lack of guidance, missed opportunities and God's directions.

I've been able to sense when God places on my heart and mind to bless others. This is a keen awareness that I am cognizant of. I sense it was imparted to me by my mother and others. I hear God speak to me and I act. I don't always act in the moment, but he will quickly remind me even if it's days later. God will bring it back to me as clear as it was the first time he placed the command in my heart.

My mother always said, "You know, our name is all we have. If you do go out there and mess that up, I don't know what to tell you." She also told me on more than one occasion, "If you get arrested, I'm going to leave you down there for a day or two." That threat alone kept me on the positive path growing up. Parents often become enablers of their children's failure and want to blame it on the system or the "man". Sometimes all it takes is to know what your parent's expectations are and what boundaries are in place.

When I think about moving from Brooklyn to Florida and learning from my dad, several thoughts come to mind. First off, he reinforced the mindset of taking advantage of opportunities and in the end my dad prepared me to be the best version of myself. He was relentless in encouraging me to take advantage of what presented itself to me. He advised me to step up to the plate and seize the time. My dad had ten kids and admonished me to take care of my family even though he didn't care for his that well. He told me he was tremendously proud of me because in his eyes, I followed in his footsteps because he was a baker, and I learned to bake. I learned to do that just from icing cakes and watching him, and I turned it into a career. He saw me married and married for a long time before he died, and he never was. He had been married once and got divorced while in the Navy, never to remarry again. He saw my long-term commitment as something to be respected and emulated. Once my daughter came along, he was so overjoyed. Maybe it was due to his having a firstborn daughter and knowing the joy it brought.

My dad and I butted heads a lot because he was trying to pour into me but didn't have the tools or skill set to do so effectively. However, he did notice I developed similar skills as he had because of his teaching I was able to create an awesome career for myself. He taught me compassion and empathy, whether he knew it or not.

Although Dad never wanted to be married, he still had a slew of kids. He saw me differently than the other kids. He was an entrepreneur with multiple income streams. He observed that I had similar interests and shared some of his traits. I learned from my dad. I learned a lot of valuable lessons from my father that early on, I didn't have an inclination to uphold. In the end, I realized he was just trying to steer me toward my best life.

When he was at the end of his life, I had to make the decision, along with one of my brothers, to pull him off a respirator because he told me that if that ever happened to him, do not keep him hooked up to any wires or life support. Now, when he said that to me, I wasn't thinking that it would come to end at all. I was prepared for his passing because we had shared our time together and grew to love and respect one another.

When I think about opportunity, leaving Brooklyn was the best decision of my life because it afforded me the time with my dad and extended family, challenging my heart and head against my dad's energy, which was drastically different than my mother's. I learned some tough lessons along the way that improved my personal tool chest of experiences, allowing me to persevere despite what society said life would be like for a young Black man growing up with a massive stigma.

In leaving the place that I loved so much, I found my wife, my soulmate, the mother of my child, and her family, whom I love dearly. They're not without their flaws, but they are a loving family. Neither family had been particularly affectionate, but we began establishing the ritual of hugging more and sharing a love language! An ex-brother-in-law had started saying "I love you" and giving a hug when arriving and departing. We advanced that wonderful change in my wife's family and ultimately, passed the ritual to all our children and they passed it on to their children. It was bittersweet when he and my sister-in-law divorced, but in the end, he imparted love in a way that had never been communicated. Our exchange feels complete, whole.

I believe the greatest expectation that you could have for yourself is to be a whole person. Be aware that life will give some tough blows, "gut shots", I call them. I've got the internal bruises, but those things make you strong and they won't kill you. It depends on how you handle it, right? Some people have the endurance for the race, and some don't. Alongside endurance, gratitude will get you far. Life presents tough blows and roses, birds, a good parking spot. To anticipate, expect, and appreciate the good out of life is a blessing that we should seek at every juncture of our journey.

Through all the moves, I did everything in my power to make sure my wife and daughter were happy. I did have a couple of occasions when I was instructed to relocate, and I refused to go. After doing a great deal of foundational work in the Tampa Bay area and creating a wonderful, award-winning region, my boss wanted to move me to Fort Lauderdale, where the grimiest stores were at that time. He wanted to deliver my polished region on a silver platter to one of his cronies. My daughter was two, and we just got her into pre-school. We had just bought a new home, and my wife was working a few miles away. This move simply could not happen.

On Monday, I expected to be kicked out of the company. But I was left in place after speaking my mind. People hire others who are like them, and I ended up counseling the new guy on how to be more empathetic and work on his temperament in order to be successful. This exchange cemented an instant connection between us.

CHAPTER 9

CHANGE AGENT IN THE WEST AND BEYOND

"A deep sense of love and belonging is an irreducible need of all people. We are biologically, cognitively, physically, and spiritually wired to love, to be loved, and to belong. When those needs are not met, we don't function as we were meant to. We break. We fall apart. We numb. We ache. We hurt others. We get sick."

—*Brené Brown, researcher and storyteller*

I WAS THE last person you would expect to be thriving in a place like Boise, Idaho.

When I became the executive national product manager and moved to Boise, it was because of a colleague who had seen my value and felt I would be the best person for the job given the changes ahead for the corporation.

There were twenty-two sales managers across the United States and about five that were slated to be his successor. At that time, I was the sixth man coming off the bench. Still, to my surprise, I received a call informing me I was now on the shortlist of candidates to be his successor. I had known the person who called for eight or nine years, and in fact, we competed for top sales, profit, and innovation honors on many occasions. It just goes to show you how authenticity, consistency, courage, and transparency can sometimes work in your favor when it's God's desire for your life. I was confident in my ability but because of the signs of the times, I didn't think they'd select the only Black person of the twenty-two sales managers to relocate to Boise.

Before I accepted the position, my colleague called me without leadership knowing, to inform me the executives were going to make the offer. He communicated that I was the candidate the executives were leaning toward because they felt I was supportive and stood up for what I believed. I knew each time I encountered these executives I was being interviewed and they paid close attention to how I managed my boss and my direct reports. During my time in the California assignment, I endured an abrasive executive who managed through fear and intimidation. The Boise executives knew of my plight to manage a working relationship with this leader and achieve corporate directives.

I believed in the corporate vision and purpose of the business. I didn't think innovations and strategic change would be detrimental to our regional business, but my direct superior, who was on a power trip and was only concerned about self-preservation. He tried to use me as a pawn to stave off changes that he didn't want to implement. I refused to participate. I believe that because the Boise executives and the colleague that recommended me saw my courage, conviction, and ability to manage up and across the organization, I was given the position.

To this day, my colleagues scratch their heads trying to figure out how and why I was selected. Honestly, I was surprised to have been selected; not that I wasn't qualified, but many of the others on that shortlist were on the inside track and were just as qualified. My gut was telling me one of them was a shoo-in. When the lot fell on me, I was skeptical and so were many colleagues.

I brought an inclusiveness that was never imagined in a non-inclusive place like that. The SVP of community affairs for the governor asked me to step in and be on the board. I worked with the mayor to change the perception of Boise and Idaho in general. That same colleague asked the governor why he didn't have anyone of color on his staff. He told her, "I've been trying." He was looking for an education policy advisor, and she called me while I was traveling and urged, "You need to get me your wife's resumé today." As I said, I listen to women!

I was involved with Juneteenth, and at the time, they had one of the oldest Black churches in the country, and we use it as a lighthouse. We wanted to extend the diversity of that church to the community at-large. We brought the old-school block party to the neighborhood where I lived and community-at-large every year. Hundreds of families attended. Companies sponsored the food and entertainment. It became a spectacular diverse event. Those five years were very productive.

At one point, the governor appointed me to the Teen Pregnancy Prevention project, and this led to several local appointments culminating in the mayor selecting me to work on the Idaho Inclusiveness Issue. When I left, I was the president of the inclusion coalition.

Diversity was an issue that the state was focused on. To be transparent, there was only a small minority population in the state. The images displayed of African Americans did not reflect our true status. The only depictions of Blacks were of the football players on the Boise state team, and my wife who was a credentialed master's degree teacher unable to even secure an interview to teach in the local school districts. Ironically, she was interviewed and hired by the governor to oversee the education for the entire state. Although she could not get a teaching position, ultimately, she was touched by godly providence to create policy and oversee curriculum for the very schools that had overlooked her talent initially.

This same situation happened again when a new leader was brought into the company. This new group vice president decided to build his own team not even considering the performance success I'd been having at the time. I believe he was insecure and intimidated because I was courageous enough to say I didn't fundamentally agree with the changes he wanted to implement.

Ultimately, his change led me to the work I'm doing today

and was the impetus I needed to move me out of my comfort zone. He was another insecure individual making his way through corporations on signing bonuses and golden parachutes. His boss, who I knew and worked for, offered me an opportunity to develop process and procedures to help small, diverse businesses become successful in working with large conglomerates. He even gave me a significant salary increase and human capital to get the program off the ground. Due to a corporate merger, the headquarters moved to Minnesota, and I was transferred there. I relocated to Minnesota with yet another culture needing to be navigated and assimilation skills coming into play to reduce anxiety.

Minnesota was a great place to live except for the long winters we had to endure, along with the spring and winter preparation that was necessary to maximize the full extent of all of the seasons. I found the office environment in Minnesota to be more inclusive as it related to the staff and middle management. There was more diversity there than I had ever seen in the corporate retail industry. The people were extremely nice and easily exemplified the "Minnesota Nice" slogan.

The company was a distribution company and overnight, they became one of the largest retailers in the country without a national diversity and inclusion strategy. A colleague and I were tapped to implement those strategies; he tackled the workforce, and I was responsible for the supplier base. Over the next five years, my team and I were able to increase spending with women and minority-owned businesses by nearly $500M and the company was recognized and celebrated for our achievements that helped the company's diversity and inclusion overall performance.

Like many acquisitions, we never experienced the synergies expected, and our performance as a company didn't meet Wall Street expectations. Therefore, another CEO was brought in to turn the company around. I believe he could've done so but wasn't given enough time. As a result, layoffs started to occur and for the first time in my career, it landed at my door.

Fortunately for me in 2012, when it happened, the company was able to take care of its obligation to officers, and I received a golden parachute. Part of my duties was to implement separation procedures for members on my team, and finally my job was eliminated.

I had already eliminated most of my team when I was charged with eliminating the remaining members. There were five left, and I was told to end their careers or leave myself. I chose the latter (although I received a great parting bonus). When cuts are needed, it seems to always affect the diversity and inclusion line on the P&L. I endured a grieving period and realized when you're with a company and a group of people for over half your life, the separation can be traumatic. It was for me! You see, I was a company man, and it never occurred to me I would be facing a layoff, but God knew.

Before my layoff, I believe God was already planning my next move. In March 2011, I moderated a panel of key executives from Coca Cola, Vlassis, and Walmart. After the panel concluded, a well-known Walmart executive complimented me and said I should consider coming to Walmart. I was flattered, to say the least, since I had been following this executive's career for many years. Ironically within the next six months, I participated at the Hispanic 360 Multicultural Conference and was approached by another key executive from Walmart, who also encouraged me to join the company.

I received my layoff notice in February 2012 and separated from the company in March 2012. I started interviewing with several different companies and had some great initial engagement. One interview I had was awesome and the organization was set to make an offer, but at the eleventh hour, they felt the job was not going to be challenging enough for me and stated they felt my "feet would go to sleep". Needless to say, I was disappointed but kept moving forward. God closed that door of opportunity and three years later, the role and department of the company were eliminated. Sometimes what seems to be a closed door can turn out to be God's favor reaching forward for your protection.

On April 7, 2012, Easter weekend, thirty days after separating from my former employer, I was scheduled to interview with Walmart. A colleague that I served on a board with, another Walmart executive invited me to her home the weekend I arrived in Arkansas. I politely declined because I didn't want to impede on her family and that occasion. However, I can't tell you how incredible it made me feel. She was one of the first executives to provide support for me when I became an associate. I knew her from our affiliation on that board in which she was the chairperson.

I served on the board of Network of Executive Women

and worked specifically with the diversity and inclusion committee. We struck up a great relationship and once I joined the company in August 2012, she became a great supporter of my work and someone I could lean on to help me navigate my way through the organization. Enough cannot be said about being authentic, allowing people to know you, and being a person of your word. I prided myself on doing the job I was assigned, especially while on that board. It allowed this executive to be open and supportive of the person she had gotten to know as we served together.

The same leader who had me take another position and had given me a considerable raise organized and lobbied for me to have the interview and ultimately the role at Walmart. He emailed me when he found out I was leaving my former employer and asked what my plans were. He helped to open the door at Walmart when he clearly didn't have to. This industry is huge, but it's frighteningly small in specific ways.

The scenario probably went something like this, "Oh, well, you know, Michael Byron is leaving the company. Why don't we invite him to join us here at Walmart? He'd make a great fit." News travels fast in the corporate world! Thirty days later, I was in Bentonville interviewing for an executive position. Unlike any interview I'd ever been through, it wasn't your normal interview. Five or six executives in the interview group, with the lowest rank being a VP, striking up a conversation rather than a formal interview. After shuffling from office to office, meeting, and having pleasantries, I was informed when my next interview would take place. In their process, they wanted to know if I would fit in the culture. This is common today.

They were trying to sell me on the community of Northwest Arkansas. They were trying to tell me why it would be good for me and my family to join the Walmart team. The executive that had invited me to her home, along with other people who I knew there, lobbied for me to consider the move. I knew several people at the corporation that had been contacted by HR to share their knowledge of my character and if they believed I could thrive in the ecosystem.

Amazingly, that executive became a sponsor for me without my ever knowing that she would be. No formalities. She spoke serendipitously on my behalf and by the time we got all the negotiations together, two and a half months later, I was working. I still wanted to continue being productive and felt I had something of value and significance to contribute. Yet who would have thought that I would land at the world's largest retailer leading one of the largest supplier diversity programs in the country months after leaving a position I was sure I would retire from?

When God gives you grace and favor, it's not necessarily for your benefit but you will reap benefits. It comes back tenfold. I was safe in the corporate environment when others offered me an opportunity. Those same businesses reached out to me to advise on projects. I have more than I can contend with right now because the cup is overflowing. I saw it in the vision before leaving.

Many of my peers sit on an island on their own. The culture allowed me to do it, but I found my way. It helped me to navigate early on. I went into Walmart trying to understand my customer, what their pain points were, what their needs were. Others didn't last in this position directly telling them what they need without that deep listening.

I think about walking into Walmart while my boss was there. I didn't want to come off as his disciple. I was two levels below him but saw him in the evening every couple of months. It was tough because they have a culture that's very specific stemming from the founder. I figured out quickly that my job was to influence a level playing field for minority suppliers. I wrote the mission and vision. After leveraging some of the leaders I had already met, I created a couple of champions to be a part of the whole spectrum of suppliers no matter their size. Sometimes you need your purpose to be reaffirmed. I like to be recognized for the work I do and the passion I bring. I helped resolve a lot of issues that had existed for a long time.

We had about 3,000 diverse suppliers (minorities, veterans, women, LGBTQ+ and people with disabilities). We were spending about $8 billion in 2012 when I joined the company and when I left 2022, we increased the spending to $14 billion. The processes we improved and the advocates we made helped exponentially. That work and my business background helped me create a technology that would show the diverse supplier's overall category performance. We created a marketing and communications plan around it, refined the website, secured a bigger budget.

Just as I tried to educate the suppliers, I had to do the

same with people internally. We possess biases as human beings, but some of those same people became champions for this work. If I had an unbeliever I would inquire, "If your sister was trying to do business with Walmart, wouldn't you want her to have an advocate?" I never tried to put them on the defense. I tried to be inclusive. We did everything from looking at the data, talking to the supplier about their performance, to then discussing their performance with the merchant. In the end, the question was, how can we help the businesses? The size and scale of our company depended on the countless relationships over the years. We had to consider cost, distribution, product to be best-in-class, and we wanted everyone to align with our desire to support diverse businesses in this country.

You're almost like an evangelist wearing a lot of different hats. A trouble shooter. One of my favorites I troubleshooted for is a supplier who makes coffee. Her son wanted to be the president overnight but didn't know the business. They brought him in as a junior executive. He didn't have a role in our meeting, but he was taking notes. I gave him a pep talk after the meeting about the family legacy, and he became a leader in the family business. I go from educating, to inspiring, motivating, and saving the day, rectifying a sizeable payment for a supplier that could've impacted their business. I get everyone together to understand the problem, we fix it overnight. It's difficult for small suppliers to get to the right person in a large organization. It's building the bridge between influence, which requires trust and credibility, and empowerment of others. In the middle is the customer, and if there are delays and disruptions in the supply chain, that's a problem—and if we have someone internally who doesn't know how to solve the problem, the communication goes dead. Problem unsolved.

Everyone knew I had their best interest at heart. When I received emails that had a negative tone, I would pick up the phone or knock on a door to fully resolve. Behind a screen, we communicate in haste; we don't proofread in the impulsive need to prove something.

We may have had unconscious biases toward small businesses because they didn't have the resources to scale like a large multinational company, but the need to make a difference was often greater. This is very personal—everyone is so busy and not all, maybe even most, take the time to pause, think it through, and legitimately help make an improvement. Emotions run high and in corporate America, if they don't ask for something a third time, it goes away. That's not a rule to live and lead by. What a way to discredit people. I want to bring people to the middle so we can solve, so we can "save money, live better." I helped write Walmart's caption on the website. The CEO said it and I tried to uphold that.

A colleague, Trudy, said fifteen years ago, "Michael, always enter a conversation in the spirit of love and be collegiate." Always assume people are going to do the right thing. When they don't, then course correct. Never go in with animosity, and usually you will get people over to your side. We have 3,000 suppliers. Time is meaning and money. Don't exclude anyone. In order to create an inclusive supply chain, everyone had a seat at the table, and we owed a thoughtful response. Size was irrelevant because every link made up the collective chain as it related to the role I had. I tried to always meet people where they are. I take into consideration who you are—there will be a personal aspect that threads all business relationships. Then you know me, you know my heart. Then I'm not coming to you for any other reason than to resolve and build relationships.

There are wonderful champions in the space. I'm better for those interactions over the course of ten years.

It seems clunky and difficult to get into Walmart or any large retail chain and sustain. We started doing wonderful work on the development side. Strategy conversations with merchants were ongoing between buyers and sellers. Where are you going? Are you capable? You need to be bold enough as an entrepreneur to ask the questions. I shouldn't be relegated to one conversation. Especially if I'm performing well. Suppliers wanted to grow fast without cultivating what they had. Then if they were apprehensive about asking of our interest in new lines or categories, I would intervene to move the conversation along. We're all here to do good and grow.

My pastor forced me into the world of retail way back when, knowing I could handle myself. Those skills translated. I have battle wounds from forty years in the industry—sometimes the scars haunt me. I had to forgive and be Michael, a genuine one, not a version with a false smile. Issues do not stop me from working with someone for common goals.

That boss told me I had interpersonal skills, and I could make a difference in inclusion. I came in as an experienced businessperson and as an advocate. He saw something in me he thought would be useful in making the company bigger. We had built so many relationships, the community came out in droves for inclusive programs. Now that I had this seat of influence, I had encounters with civil rights icons John Lewis and Elijah Cummings, who both encouraged me to use my seat for good and never waste a day of it. Each encounter was during a Black History Month event. It reaffirmed what I already knew, lighting a fire under me. I always had it in me to do what's right for people. This is not relegated to my race; this is anybody that is perceived underutilized, not able to have the seat at the table, I go to bat for them. I've had injustices happen. Through God's grace, they worked themselves out. Somehow, a change or a clear path.

There are different parts of inclusion. I'm living proof of inclusion. As I look at where I am and what people are seeking help with, it's supplier inclusion, overall strategy and communication. You need to have inclusion in your supply chain, not simply your internal nucleus. I started asking diverse suppliers to report their inclusion activities—I wanted them to know I had the same expectations for small or large companies. From those conversations spawned advocacy. If you're a CEO, you're as important as any other CEO, whether you lead five or 5 million employees. Ask for what you need from those who promote inclusion in the public domain; this is really when you discover what brands are authentic. Preparation is paramount. Anticipate what your customers will ask. Spend 100 hours researching, preparing, and developing your pitch. In most case, if you're lucky, this is a thirty-minute meeting. I check clients' emails to be sure the communication is the right tone and message.

Who's to say the next person I encounter won't become a Sam Walton. I've partnered with a lot of entrepreneurs who have soared. I've sat on a lot of boards and created numerous minority programs. I believe that you must do more than have a chicken dinner and give out award certificates—you must teach people how to do this! The one-shot meetings are no joke. Inclusivity needs to happen. Supplier diversity started in the automotive industry in the late 1960s when women and people of color could not get contracts. We're still talking about inequity. It's about using your seat of influence and not being afraid. Sometimes it costs you, but I never questioned, never knew what it cost. I focused on how my seat of influence could help someone.

CHAPTER 10

PASSING IT ON

> "Love does not begin and end the way
> we seem to think it does. Love is a battle,
> love is a war; love is a growing up."
>
> —*James Baldwin, novelist*

WHEN I THINK about all those steps to take me from Brooklyn to Boise, I now realize that every one of them was calculated, they were orchestrated. Some of what transpired along the way seemed like it was designed to destroy me. Yet I realize in hindsight it was the divine orienting things to happen so that at key moments I could benefit, and so benefit others.

All the love and lessons shaped who I am. As of this writing, in men's ministry, we're studying the "Kingdom Man", which has made me look back on the tapestry of people along my journey and noting where I made an impact. I want every interaction to make a solid imprint that doesn't fade away.

Every smile, every greeting, and every moment of kind-ness contributes to a tapestry of human connection that enriches our lives and the lives of others. So, as I reflect on my journey, I strive to make kindness a priority. In a world that can sometimes feel heavy and indifferent, I choose to be a beacon of warmth, knowing that my actions, no matter how small, can create waves of change in the lives of others. After all, it is in these moments of connection that we truly find our purpose and the profound impact we can have on each other's lives.

I'm reminded of gentlemen that helped build one of my homes during my journey from Brooklyn to Boise, and beyond. As you know, when building a home there can be lots of delays, miscommunication, and many other calam-ities. Because of our patience and generosity, he said to us, "Mr. and Mrs. Byron, you are the salt of the earth," and I have held that statement in my heart for the past thirteen years. Similarly, I have saved the "Salt and Light" expressions of gratitude by way of personal notes, emails, and thank-you cards throughout my career. I have carried them in my "Love Box" from one location and assignment to the next. When I needed inspiration or reassurance that I was doing the right thing, wow, this treasure of expressions reinforced my quote, "Walk in your purpose and be intentional in action." Recently, I heard the pleasure of hearing this passage being used in a message.

Matthew 5:13-16 / Salt and Light: (13) "You are the salt of the earth. But if the salt loses its saltiness, how can it be made salty again? It is no longer good for anything, except to be thrown out and trampled underfoot." (14) "You are the light of the world. A town built on a hill cannot be hidden. (15) Neither do people light a lamp and put it under a bowl. Instead, they put it on its stand, and it gives light to everyone in the house. (16) In the same way, let your light shine before others, that they may see your good deeds and glorify your Father in heaven.

From the Love Box—"Salt and Light" Expressions That Lifted Me

It is always a delight seeing you and Wednesday was no exception. I'm delighted to see you've settled comfortably in Bentonville. Your transition is such a wonderful lesson that flexibility, and a willingness to accept change, pave the road to opportunity. Please accept my best wishes for your continued personal success and professional prosperity.

Great meeting you. Always good to see another Brooklyn boy from the neighborhood who has done good, and who is making a difference. You are keeping alive the Brooklyn motto, "When we roll, we roll hard."

I would like to express my sincere appreciation for selecting [us] in the Walmart Tuck University MBE scholarship program. Attending this program has been absolutely life changing. I have learned so much about the different areas of my business and how to make improvements. Most of all, the importance of serving the community. I am inspired to work even harder each day to bring about great change.

I wanted to say hello and give you a quick update on our progress with Walmart. We are in the early stages but are ramped up and ready. I believe four orders have been placed with so far. Things are looking good so far and we are hoping for a good transition. Thank you for the business, if it weren't for our networking events this contract would not have happened. We will have a great story to tell about how our customer introduced us to you at your previous job. You remembered introduced us to the right people at Walmart. Networking always pays off in the end, you just don't know who or when.

On behalf of the small and diverse businesses you assist daily— THANK YOU! Your support of our business with information and guidance provides the foundation for our growth and development. Always remember your efforts, make our world a better place!

The majority of senior directors go to work and go home. The majority of people engage in activities that are self-serving. It is evident you are not the majority; it is likely many people will experience a better quality of life because of your willingness to share your time, knowledge, and resources with Veteran Edge conference in Dallas. You're a rock star!

I love your passion about inclusion. It's clearly your fire and what makes you so special. You connected with everyone last night. You made inclusion seem so easy and yet in the real world, we know it's not so easily observed. I loved the phrase "I can be inclusive by including all people in all things." Inclusion is about trust and relationships. While I think I am pretty good in this area, this is a key area for me to continue working on both personally and professionally and across my area.

I am a junior marketing major at Howard University, and I was part of the inaugural group of interns at the Bentonville Film Festival 2017. It was a pleasure meeting you this week and wanted to thank you for taking time to have brunch with us and really embracing us as interns. I could see that you genuinely cared, and it meant so much to have the support. I appreciate it more than you know. You gave a lot of great advice, that I will definitely take heed to. I love what you're doing with Walmart and connecting them with minority-owned businesses. I hope my work in the future is just as fulfilling. Your story was inspirational, and I hope to make as great of an impact as you some day, and thank you for brunch also, that was so nice of you.

All of the conversations we've had these last few months have really lit a fire in me, and I find myself paying attention to more and more to nuances in conversations, presentations, formal and informal events I didn't before…and even though I felt like there was undeniable inequality before we started meeting, I feel like I'm starting to see what it actually looks like playing out in real time. I really appreciate your willingness to spend time with me and share your wisdom and experience…it's been incredibly valuable. Looking forward to continuing to work together.

Michael, most importantly, I want you to know how much it meant to my son Joseph to meet you and hear you speak. You're inspirational. He is young man trying to find his way. As you know, there are highs and lows of owning a small business. But after speaking with you, he left feeling like he can do this.

Words cannot express how grateful I am for your support, mentorship and friendship. Who knows what could have happened if I didn't get the extra pitch practice before the competition! I really appreciate the opportunity to sit at the Walmart table amongst such successful and experienced individuals.

This morning, I woke up to pictures of our snack mix on the shelf at Walmart. It was like a dream come true. Honestly, I have customers. I am so happy to be working with you and your team.

Everyone's Economy

Now that I have evolved from Corporate America, I have been asked to share my career experiences as a retailer, merchant, operator, people leader, convener and connector, board member, speaker, and advocate. I am thrilled and appreciative of the many opportunities I have been given to share those experiences and skills to further address how we can and must address the wealth gap in this country. In reflecting on my journey further, I realize that each role I have held was a unique chapter that contributed to my understanding of the complexities of our economic landscape.

From the bustling aisles of retail, where I learned the importance of customer connection and the nuances of consumer behavior, to the strategic boardroom discussions that shaped corporate policies, each experience has equipped me with valuable insights. As a people leader, I discovered the profound impact of mentorship and community building, understanding that the strength of any organization lies in its people. I have witnessed firsthand how genuine connections can empower individuals and transform lives, creating a ripple effect that extends far beyond the workplace.

As I step into the role of a speaker and advocate, I carry

with me not only my successes but also the lessons learned from challenges faced along the way. It is this blend of triumph and adversity that fuels my passion for addressing the wealth gap—a disparity that affects not only individuals and families but the very fabric of our society. I believe that by sharing my story and engaging in meaningful conversations, we can inspire collective action towards a more equitable future.

I envision a dialogue that transcends boundaries, inviting voices from all walks of life to contribute to this critical conversation. Together, we can explore innovative solutions that bridge the gap, fostering an environment where opportunities are accessible to everyone, regardless of their background. This mission is not just a personal endeavor; it is a call to action for us all, as we strive to create a world where economic disparity becomes a relic of the past. With each story shared and every connection made, we move closer to a future that honors the dignity and potential of every individual.

I am indeed, walking in my purpose and being intentional in my actions.

ABOUT THE AUTHOR

Before joining Walmart in 2012, Michael Byron served as Vice President of Supplier Diversity at SUPERVALU, Inc., a U.S. wholesale and retail grocer with annual sales of $44 billion and 180,000 employees. While at SUPERVALU, Michael increased the number of diverse suppliers by 5 to 10% annually and added $425 million in supply chain spending with diverse-owned businesses.

Also, Michael worked at Albertsons, a U.S. grocer, as the Corporate Merchandising and Operations Director, directly impacting the bottom line through strong business aptitude and visionary leadership. Michael and his team increased market revenue significantly by launching innovative merchandising strategies within the retail industry. As a result, in 2002 Michael was voted by *Supermarket News* magazine as one of top 50 bakery operators in the U.S.

As a recognized industry leader, Michael has been a Sought-after speaker and panelist, most notably as the keynote speaker for the Hispanic 360 Conference, Association of National Advertisers, Latino Coalition Legislative Summit, Midwest Minority Supplier Develop Council Business Opportunity Fair, as well as Executive Sponsor and C-Suite Moderator for The Network of Executive Women's Multicultural Business Forum. Michael is consistently recognized as a passionate collaborator, speaker, and panelist for his business acumen as a former retail and operation's leader. He's received numerous personal and professional awards for his work in business and advancing supply chain inclusion.

Michael holds a Bachelor of Science in business management and executive retail management and leadership certifications from Cornell University and the University of Phoenix.